A CENTURY *of*
GRIMSBY

'Jimmy' Whitcombe, son of Skipper Jim Whitcombe (see p. 55), holding on to a DF (Directional Finding) aerial on top of the bridge of a trawler. (*Opposite*) 'Jimmy' Whitcombe, dressed for a night on the town.

A CENTURY *of*
GRIMSBY

DAVID CUPPLEDITCH

First published in 2000 by Sutton Publishing Limited

This new paperback edition first published in 2007 by
Sutton Publishing

Reprinted in 2011 by
The History Press
The Mill, Brimscombe Port,
Stroud, Gloucestershire, GL5 2QG
www.thehistorypress.co.uk

Reprinted 2012

British Library Cataloguing in Publication Data
A catalogue record for this book is available from the British Library.

ISBN 978-0-7509-4919-4

Front endpaper: Turn-of-the-century view of the fishing dock.
Back endpaper: Every other traditional British industry that has been
decimated in the post-war era has been given compensation except
for the fishing industry, but as I write this fishermen are finally to be
awarded their just dues – twenty-four years late! After the demise of the
long-haul trawlers, the last eleven 'Cat' class British United Trawlers
were sold in 1985. Only the seine-netters and middle distance boats were
left to carry on fishing.
Half title page: Great Grimsby crest.

> *This book is dedicated to the memory of*
> *Jessie Altoft (1942–78), who lived on the*
> *Yarborough Estate in the 1960s and who*
> *died tragically at the age of 36.*

Typeset in Photina.
Typesetting and origination by
Sutton Publishing Limited.
Printed and bound in England.

The Siena Tower, Italy, upon which
the designs for the Dock Tower were
based.

Contents

The life of a fisherman was hard and dangerous. Between the wars, when the sea was free from exclusion zones, a Grimsby trawler could steam up to Bear Island (the trip, then, took nearly a week). Once it dropped its nets and trawled, the crew had to gut the fish, pack it in ice and store it in the 'fish hole' in two hours, before the next catch came up. This continuous process went on night and day until the boat was fully laden and the crew could return to port. One of the perks when gutting the fish was to retain the liver, which was then liquidised and eventually turned into cod liver oil. The crew were paid separately for this and it became a bonus on top of their wages.

Foreword

BY AUSTIN MITCHELL MP

ALL GRIMSBY LIFE IS HERE, BEAUTIFULLY ILLUSTRATED BY DAVID CUPPLEDITCH'S WONDERFUL PHOTOGRAPHS OF OUR LAST CENTURY. HE'S DONE A GREAT SERVICE, NOT JUST FOR GRIMSBY FOLK WHO'RE ALWAYS PROUD OF THEIR GREAT LITTLE TOWN, BUT ALSO FOR A WORLD OUTSIDE WHICH DESERVES TO KNOW WHAT A REAL COMMUNITY WITH REAL PEOPLE IS LIKE.

My predecessor as MP, Tony Crosland, always took Grimsby as his touchstone for the real world. So do I. It's never frenetic with fashion or obsessed with ephemera, but preoccupied with the basics: jobs, development and community. Life isn't impersonal like the big cities. Grimsby is a community which has its priorities right.

Life is good in Grimsby but never easy as David's photographs show. Proudly patriotic, it's made more than its fair share of sacrifices in war. It began the twentieth century as a one-industry town. Fishing was always the toughest and riskiest British industry but it supported a unique way of life in the Marsh's terraces and the man's world of 'down dock'. In good times it generated high earnings for fishermen and big profits for owners and merchants, though far too little of that was ploughed back into the civic ornaments, buildings and institutions with which wealth adorned other northern towns.

As the place where the riches of the sea and those of the soil of fertile Lincolnshire meet, Grimsby developed food processing to become Europe's Food Town whence food for the millions flowed out. Postwar, a wise council diversified by developing the Humber Bank for chemical and petroleum industries. The trading opportunities from the mighty Humber grew as Britain's trade axis moved from west to east, from Atlantic and Commonwealth to Europe. We are the gateway to Europe and Immingham is the Jewel in the Crown of the nation's docks.

Out of all this Grimsby built a unique community brought to vivid life in this collection. Yet success has come neither massively nor easily. Grimsby has always struggled against the elements, isolation and brutal economic forces. The loss of distant water fishing opportunities after Iceland's 200 mile limit and the refusal of the EU to allow us to rebuild the industry within our own waters was a bitter blow. A unique way of life was destroyed with that proud industry.

So Grimsby found the resulting problems of low wages, high unemployment and social deprivation with minimal help from government, in the form of regional aid and grants, but a great deal of local effort and ingenuity. This bootstrap generation gave us the new landing company, the new market and fish docks, the Top Town Shopping Centre, the development of Alexander Dock, the Fishing Heritage Centre and the Auditorium, all a determined effort to diversify which has brought new industries, though never enough.

Development is a constant struggle though its fruits are seen in this book and in a community which has shifted away from the docks, a town life which has spread out from the crowded terraces and from Hainton Square and Freeman Street to the central shopping areas, the suburbs and the surrounding villages, and to a new diversity and entertainment. All strengthen Grimsby's claim to be, not the richest of northern communities, but one of the best to live, work and to invest in.

When first elected as its Borough Member, I became heir to a tradition going back to the first Grimsby MPs at the end of the thirteenth century: indeed, to some I now seem to have been one of them. Today, after the constant changes in local and regional government, I represent part of the larger authority of North East Lincolnshire. Yet its core is Grimsby and the town remains the best of communities with more common identity and local pride than bigger, more metropolitan conurbations. Don't just take my word for it. You'll see it in this fascinating collection of photos of the real life, real people and real characters which brightened our last century. The past may be black and white in the photographic archives but it was vivid and colourful in Grimsby, and David Cuppleditch's excellent selection of photographs makes it live again in all its colour and uniqueness.

It is unlikely that this practice would be tolerated today. The workman is lowered on a rope while working on the Dock Tower.

Britain: A Century
of Change

Two women encumbered with gas masks go about their daily tasks during
the early days of the war. (*Hulton Getty Picture Collection*)

The sixty years ending in 1900 were a period of huge transformation for Britain. Railway stations, post-and-telegraph offices, police and fire stations, gasworks and gasometers, new livestock markets and covered markets, schools, churches, football grounds, hospitals and asylums, water pumping stations and sewerage plants totally altered the urban scene, and the country's population tripled with more than seven out of ten people being born in or moving to the towns. The century that followed, leading up to the Millennium's end in 2000, was to be a period of even greater change.

When Queen Victoria died in 1901, she was measured for her coffin by her grandson Kaiser Wilhelm, the London prostitutes put on black mourning and the blinds came down in the villas and terraces spreading out from the old town centres. These centres were reachable by train and tram, by the new bicycles and still newer motor cars, were connected by the new telephone, and lit by gas or even electricity. The shops may have been full of British-made cotton and woollen clothing but the grocers and butchers were selling cheap Danish bacon, Argentinian beef, Australasian mutton and tinned or dried fish and fruit from Canada, California and South Africa. Most of these goods were carried in British-built-and-crewed ships burning Welsh steam coal.

As the first decade moved on, the Open Spaces Act meant more parks, bowling greens and cricket pitches. The First World War transformed the place of women, as they took over many men's jobs. Its other legacies were the war memorials which joined the statues of Victorian worthies in main squares round the land. After 1918 death duties and higher taxation bit hard, and a quarter of England changed hands in the space of only a few years.

The multiple shop – the chain store – appeared in the high street: Sainsburys, Maypole, Lipton's, Home & Colonial, the Fifty Shilling Tailor, Burton, Boots, W.H. Smith. The shopper was spoilt for choice, attracted by the brash fascias and advertising hoardings for national brands like Bovril, Pears Soap, and Ovaltine. Many new buildings began to be seen, such as garages, motor showrooms, picture palaces (cinemas), 'palais de dance', and ribbons of 'semis' stretched along the roads and new bypasses and onto the new estates nudging the green belts.

During the 1920s cars became more reliable and sophisticated as well as commonplace, with developments like the electric self-starter making them easier for women to drive. Who wanted to turn a crank handle in the new short skirt? This was, indeed, the electric age as much as the motor era. Trolley buses, electric trams and trains extended mass transport and electric light replaced gas in the street and the home, which itself was groomed by the vacuum cleaner.

A major jolt to the march onward and upward was administered by the Great Depression of the early 1930s. The older British industries

– textiles, shipbuilding, iron, steel, coal – were already under pressure from foreign competition when this worldwide slump arrived. Luckily there were new diversions to alleviate the misery. The 'talkies' arrived in the cinemas; more and more radios and gramophones were to be found in people's homes; there were new women's magazines, with fashion, cookery tips and problem pages; football pools; the flying feats of women pilots like Amy Johnson; the Loch Ness Monster; cheap chocolate and the drama of Edward VIII's abdication.

Things were looking up again by 1936 and new light industry was booming in the Home Counties as factories struggled to keep up with the demand for radios, radiograms, cars and electronic goods, including the first television sets. The threat from Hitler's Germany meant rearmament, particularly of the airforce, which stimulated aircraft and aero engine firms. If you were lucky and lived in the south, there was good money to be earned. A semi-detached house cost £450, a Morris Cowley £150. People may have smoked like chimneys but life expectancy, since 1918, was up by 15 years while the birth rate had almost halved.

In some ways it is the little memories that seem to linger longest from the Second World War: the kerbs painted white to show up in the

A W.H.Smith shop front in Beaconsfield, 1922.

11

blackout, the rattle of ack-ack shrapnel on roof tiles, sparrows killed by bomb blast. The biggest damage, apart from London, was in the south-west (Plymouth, Bristol) and the Midlands (Coventry, Birmingham). Postwar reconstruction was rooted in the Beveridge Report which set out the expectations for the Welfare State. This, together with the nationalisation of the Bank of England, coal, gas, electricity and the railways, formed the programme of the Labour government in 1945.

Times were hard in the late 1940s, with rationing even more stringent than during the war. Yet this was, as has been said, 'an innocent and well-behaved era'. The first let-up came in 1951 with the Festival of Britain and there was another fillip in 1953 from the Coronation, which incidentally gave a huge boost to the spread of TV. By 1954 leisure motoring had been resumed but the Comet – Britain's best hope for taking on the American aviation industry – suffered a series of mysterious crashes. The Suez debacle of 1956 was followed by an acceleration in the withdrawal from Empire, which had begun in 1947 with the Independence of India. Consumerism was truly born with the advent of commercial TV and most homes soon boasted washing machines, fridges, electric irons and fires.

Children collecting aluminium to help the war effort, London, 1940s. (*IWM*)

The *Lady Chatterley* obscenity trial in 1960 was something of a straw in the wind for what was to follow in that decade. A collective loss of inhibition seemed to sweep the land, as the Beatles and the Rolling Stones transformed popular music, and retailing, cinema and the theatre were revolutionised. Designers, hairdressers, photographers and models moved into places vacated by an Establishment put to flight by the new breed of satirists spawned by *Beyond the Fringe* and *Private Eye*.

A street party to celebrate the Queen's Coronation, June 1953. (*Hulton Getty Picture Collection*)

In the 1970s Britain seems to have suffered a prolonged hangover after the excesses of the previous decade. Ulster, inflation and union troubles were not made up for by entry into the EEC, North Sea Oil, Women's Lib or, indeed, Punk Rock. Mrs Thatcher applied the corrective in the 1980s, as the country moved more and more from its old manufacturing base over to providing services, consulting, advertising, and expertise in the 'invisible' market of high finance or in IT.

The post-1945 townscape has seen changes to match those in the worlds of work, entertainment and politics. In 1952 the Clean Air Act served notice on smogs and pea-souper fogs, smuts and blackened buildings, forcing people to stop burning coal and go over to smokeless sources of heat and energy. In the same decade some of the best urban building took place in the 'new towns' like Basildon, Crawley, Stevenage and Harlow. Elsewhere open warfare was declared on slums and what was labelled inadequate, cramped, back-to-back, two-up, two-down, housing. The new 'machine for living in' was a flat in a high-rise block. The architects and planners who promoted these were in league with the traffic engineers, determined to keep the motor car moving whatever the price in multi-storey car parks, meters, traffic wardens and ring roads. The old pollutant, coal smoke, was replaced by petrol and diesel exhaust, and traffic noise.

Fast food was no longer only a pork pie in a pub or fish-and-chips. There were Indian curry houses, Chinese take-aways and American-style hamburgers, while the drinker could get away from beer in a wine bar. Under the impact of television the big Gaumonts and Odeons closed or were rebuilt as multi-screen cinemas, while the palais de dance gave way to discos and clubs.

Punk rockers demonstrate their anarchic style during the 1970s. (*Barnaby's Picture Library*)

From the late 1960s the introduction of listed buildings and conservation areas, together with the growth of preservation societies, put a brake on 'comprehensive redevelopment'. The end of the century and the start of the Third Millennium see new challenges to the health of towns and the wellbeing of the nine out of ten people who now live urban lives. The fight is on to prevent town centres from dying, as patterns of housing and shopping change, and edge-of-town supermarkets exercise the attractions of one-stop shopping. But as banks and department stores close, following the haberdashers, greengrocers, butchers and ironmongers, there are signs of new growth such as farmers' markets, and corner stores acting as pick-up points where customers collect shopping ordered on-line from web sites.

Futurologists tell us that we are in stage two of the consumer revolution: a shift from mass consumption to mass customisation driven by

Millennium celebrations over the Thames
at Westminster, New Year's Eve, 1999.
(*Barnaby's Picture Library*)

a desire to have things that fit us and our particular lifestyle exactly,
and for better service. This must offer hope for small city-centre shop
premises, as must the continued attraction of physical shopping,
browsing and being part of a crowd: in a word, 'shoppertainment'.
Another hopeful trend for towns is the growth in the number of young
people postponing marriage and looking to live independently, alone,
where there is a buzz, in 'swinging single cities'. Theirs is a 'flats-and-
cafés' lifestyle, in contrast to the 'family suburbs', and certainly fits in
with government's aim of building 60 per cent of the huge amount of
new housing needed on 'brown' sites, recycled urban land. There looks
to be plenty of life in the British town yet.

Grimsby: An Introduction

Grimsby made a huge contribution to Britain's wealth in the twentieth century. Indeed, one could be forgiven for saying that that's what put the 'Great' into Grimsby. Notwithstanding the sacrifice which many Grimbarian families made during the First World War (not just the bravery of men at the Front – the docks were used as a naval base, old warehouses were turned into munitions factories and the financial toll was met without question), in the 1920s and '30s, despite terrible conditions brought on by the General Strike and the Depression, Grimsby still pulled through with optimistic resolve. Even during the Second World War, when the town was blitzed, Grimbarians developed a special camaraderie to combat Hitler's bombs with cheerful stoicism. However, it was in the postwar period that things began to go wrong.

At the start of the twentieth century Grimsby was the most important fishing port in the UK. By its close we saw a port much diminished in size and, like British industry (or what is left of it), operating at half-cock, despite a massive recent investment in the fishing docks complex. It would be easy to blame successive governments and they must shoulder their share of the blame, but it is not principally their fault. It is a combination of human greed with extended territorial waters covering traditional fishing grounds and massive over-fishing on a hitherto unthought-of scale. These factors have brought Britain's fishing industry almost to a halt.

Back in the 1950s, when Grimsby fishermen earned good money, there was a buzz around the town which filtered through to a host of ancillary services such as specialist shops, photographers, craftsmen, cinemas, restaurants and pubs. When Harold Macmillan said that 'some of our people have never had it so good', he could easily have been referring to Grimsby. The 'Cod War' of 1958–60 was the first inkling that all was not well. But when redevelopment took place in the early 1960s the heart of the town was removed. Shops like Duke's in Bethlehem Street, with its smell of carbolic mixed with creosote, were demolished for road widening while whole streets were wiped out

Seine-netters still operate out of Grimsby. This photograph was taken c. 1975.

15

as a package of slum clearance in favour of high-rise flats. The Old Market Place lost its Corn Exchange, and Chambers' Tudor Café – with its uniformed waitresses serving afternoon tea and scones while the 'Palm Court Trio' played – closed shortly after. Even Guy & Smith's, Grimsby's prestige store which attracted customers from all over the county, succumbed to a take-over.

The fervour with which old Grimsby was torn down can be attributed to events like the Festival of Britain in 1951, when everyone was mesmerised by those garish colours, innovative designs and '50s architecture. Wasn't there also a dome at that Exhibition on the South Bank? By the time these ideas reached Grimsby, everyone was convinced that they must be right. The zeal with which local planners implemented them was remorseless and it is only recently, when the rest of us have said 'hold on a minute', that a more objective view has been taken about what should and should not be pulled down.

As a final insult, Great Grimsby had its borders removed in 1974, leaving Lincolnshire to become part of the newly formed Humberside. No Grimbarian worth his salt (if you'll excuse the pun) wanted to be part of Humberside and it was only after continual barracking and lobbying that Grimsby reverted to its traditional roots. It returned to Lincolnshire in 1996 but, instead of rejoining the umbrella of Lincolnshire County Council, formed its own council of North East Lincolnshire.

In the course of the twentieth century Grimsby produced a host of individual characters, some of whom are seen within these pages. It absorbed an influx of Russian emigrés fleeing the Revolution, some of whom stayed and settled in West Marsh, which soon acquired the nickname of 'Little Russia'. Then there were Scandinavians, with names like Nielsen, Evinson and Olsen, echoing Grimsby's history from the time of the Vikings. In more recent times the Findus company had a factory here, and Christian Salvesen still operate in the area. Grimsby has spawned sons with international reputations like Ross (from J. Carl Ross) and Harry Ramsden to the eccentric 'Two-Stick Charlie', who enacted impersonations of Napoleon and Charlie Chaplin in the Old Market Place during the 1920s and '30s.

In the late 1950s and early '60s there was the Hacienda Bar, Grimsby's first real coffee bar and a great meeting place. It was followed by the Salamander, in Grimsby Road, Cleethorpes, which took on its mantle. Then there was Reinecke's, in Freeman Street, which specialised in soft drinks, and Cox's famous fish and chip shop off Central Market, known as 'The Peabung'. There has always been a range of Grimsby pubs to choose from, not least the Honest Lawyer (a contradiction in terms?) in Kent Street, which was demolished in 1964 by the old Grimsby Corporation.

There have been a number of books on Grimsby in recent years and most of them have relied heavily on pictorial documentation or photographs. The camera does not lie and presents an accurate image as opposed to the written word, which can be misinterpreted. Many historians are now realising this. It is hoped that this new volume will make a useful addition and give as much pleasure to those who read it as it has to the author who compiled it.

The Start of the Century

1901 The famous Grimsby '1901 Lock-Out'.

1900 On 19 May Mafeking was relieved and Baden-Powell became a national hero. There was much rejoicing up and down England at this high point in an otherwise difficult war. Children were given a half day's holiday. To celebrate Mafeking there was a procession in Victoria Street, although the relief of Ladysmith is probably better remembered in Grimsby by the naming of Ladysmith Road.

1901 For fourteen weeks the 'Lock-Out' caused immense hardship to fishermen and their families. It led to a full-scale riot and prompted the despatch of three naval gunboats. The dispute centred on the trawler-owners' decision to pay crews a share-wage from the catch rather than a weekly wage. Up to this point only skippers and mates were paid by this method but not the crew. While the lock-out was in progress no ship could leave port because the boats were packed like sardines.

1901 This football match between Grimsby All Saints and Sheffield took place at Blundell Park. It was said that the All Saints team was a stepping stone to the more celebrated Grimsby Town side. It was also the first year that Blundell Park was used as a football ground.

1911 The first Town football team had been formed back in 1879. This is the 1911/12 Grimsby Town Football Club team, photographed by the Lowthian Brothers of 146 Freeman Street. The team comprised of: (forwards) Staniforth, Hubbard, Mounteney, Mayson and Worth; (half-backs) Browell, Gordon and Martin; (backs) Wheelhouse and Arrowsmith; (goalie) Lonsdale. It was this team that redeemed Grimsby's pride by playing 38 matches and winning 25 of them. In the 1910/11 season, Grimsby Town had played 38 matches and only won nine.

1907 The Channel Fleet, under Admiral Lord Charles Beresford, came to Grimsby in this year. Front row, centre section (left to right): George Doughty MP, The Rt Hon. Lord Heneage, Admiral Beresford, Mayor Jacob Pickwell, Captain Sturdee and the Mayor of Hull, Alderman H. Feldman. In the right-hand section is the equally unmistakable figure of G.L. Alward (the trawler owner), standing in the centre of the second row with top hat, moustache and goatee beard. It was Alward who collaborated with Beresford to turn Grimsby trawlers into auxiliary minesweepers during the First World War. Next to Alward is Militia Officer Captain Ernest Sleight (heavily moustached) and, just visible in the back row, T.G. Tickler. Inside the Mayor's Parlour, behind the window, Lady Doughty (with hat) can be seen looking over the group, which was photographed by G.H. Greenwood of 36 Hainton Avenue.

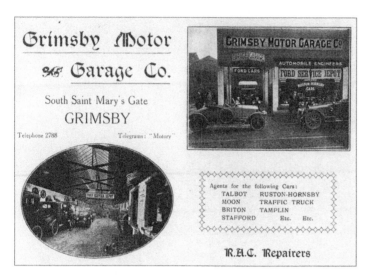

1907 Probably the biggest change in this century to the way people lived lay with transport. The advent of the motor-carriage which was to replace its more traditional rival, horse-drawn traffic, was the key. This was the Grimsby Motor & Garage Company's advertisement. The famous Lloyd cars were made in the town, in Patrick Street; these are now collectors' items.

1907 Herbert Stephenson was one of the first Grimsby traders to take advantage of this new mode of transport. His Darracq lorry took pride of place outside his florist's shop in Old Market, although this picture was taken outside the family home in Brighowgate.

1910 In January Tom Wing (left), the Liberal candidate, beat Sir George Doughty, the Conservative MP, at the polls by 322 votes. Lloyd George (centre), who appeared and spoke on his behalf, may have tipped the balance. It was to be a brief sitting. Only ten months later, in November, the redoubtable Doughty reclaimed his seat. The photograph was taken outside Fryston House, Bargate, and Sir Francis Bennett is on the right.

1910 Sir George Doughty had been Grimsby's MP since 1896, first as a Liberal then as a Conservative. The son of a coal merchant, he left school at thirteen and was apprenticed to John Brown, who built the Town Hall, Royal Hotel and St Andrew's Church. By the age of twenty-four he had his own building firm and at thirty-six was the largest owner of leased housing in West Marsh. He founded the *Telegraph* (later the *Grimsby Evening Telegraph*) and was responsible for the Doughty Museum. He died in 1914.

1912 Grimsby Bowling Club was started in April 1887, electing Mr J. Sutcliffe as its first President. A plot of land in Brighowgate was purchased, a substantial pavilion erected and J. Brigham selected as groundsman.

1912   1912 marked the visit of King George V and Queen Mary on 22 July primarily to open the new Immingham Dock, but also the Children's Mission. Crowds turned out that day to catch a glimpse of the royal couple.

1912   The funeral of William Grange (1821–1912), at the George Street Wesleyan Chapel, reflected the warmth and respect which the people of Grimsby felt towards their venerable Town Clerk. Streets were lined with mourners wishing to pay their last respects to the man who was reputedly the oldest Town Clerk in England. William Grange was a staunch Methodist, a teetotaller and had held the position of Town Clerk for fifty-one years! He was buried in Scartho Road cemetery.

Up to the First World War music hall enjoyed its heyday. Grimsby's own contralto, Ethel Stephenson (seen here), gave many fine performances. Later in life she married the violinist George Hancock, who often accompanied her in recital.

We also tend to forget the many craftsmen who abounded in that era. This was Fred Popple, who made violins, photographed by H. Jancowski of 3 Market Place.

Children were brought up to be seen and not heard, as this delightful photo of Wintringham Secondary Day School girls portrays.

1914 The day after Sir George Doughty's funeral his successor was announced: it was to be the celebrated jam manufacturer, T.G. Tickler, who served the town from 1914 to 1919. Tickler had factories in Grimsby and Southall, London, while his fruit farms lay in Lincolnshire at Laceby and Bradley.

Doughty's opponent, the Liberal candidate, was the trawler owner Alf Bannister, who amassed a fortune from his fleet of *Saxon* boats. The one-time 'Trawler King' lived at Saxon House in St Peter's Avenue, Cleethorpes. His old home has been turned into the Saxon House Hotel, run by former Grimsby Town football player Harry Wainman.

If Herbert Sephenson had to choose between the more traditional horse-drawn conveyance and the new-fangled motor car, there is no doubt which he would have chosen. Here we see two of his children, Frank and Gladys, in this early version of a Reliant Robin three-wheeler!

The Palace Theatre Music Hall opened in 1904 with its adjoining Palace Buffet, which still survives. When the popularity of the Music Hall waned, it was transformed into a cinema in 1931 until 1943 when it reverted to its use as a theatre after the bombing of the old Tivoli.

This turn-of-the-century photograph was taken at the Eleanor Street site of Grimsby Municipal College (later Wintringham Grammar School) showing the staff under the headmastership of Mr Stream.

1912 When this advert appeared, Guy & Smith Ltd were making considerable additions to their premises. They were taking over the premises of Smith & Sons (dressmakers, furriers and drapers) at 9 and 11 Victoria Street, David Smith's (house furnishers, tailors, silk mercers and undertakers – and no relation) at 13 and 15 and Whitlam Smith's ironmongery business at no. 17, which became Guy & Smith's ironmongery department. All these additions made it the most prestigious store in Grimsby, a reputation it held until 1969 when the House of Fraser group bought the premises and re-named the store Binns. Note the cobbles down Victoria Street – these were to be replaced by tarmacadam at a later date.

1908 This is Murray Street on Grimsby Fish Docks and the railway line is the original main line from the Dock Station to Cleethorpes. The building in the background is still there and, for many years, was the offices of the North Eastern Steam Fishing Co. Ltd. The rulley in this picture was used to transport fish crates and was photographed by Sid Burton of Cleethorpe Road, Grimsby.

This was the staff of the Fish Docks Railway, which had its own Dock Master (seated in the centre of the group). The Royal Dock also had its own Dock Master.

Of all the portraits in this book, this one of Edward Bannister (1821–1916) is my favourite. Whatever he lacks in looks is made up for in character. He was a far-sighted businessman who perceived that coal would be essential for trawlers. Before the turn of the century many fishing boats had relied on sail. He became a very wealthy man; one of his principal customers was the Admiralty.

BUNKER COAL
For Steam Trawlers

Household COAL
AND
Steam Coal

Weight and Quality
Guaranteed

Entire Wagons Supplied at
Wholesale Prices

Edw. BANNISTER & Co., Ltd.

FITTERS TO THE ADMIRALTY,

Coal Exporters : GRIMSBY

Shipping Office: ROYAL DOCK CHAMBERS

Telegrams: "Bannister, Grimsby."   Tel. No. 626 Adam Smith Street

	Foremen
CRESSEY STREET — — —	W. Brothwell
RAILWAY STREET *(Dock Station)* —	J. Young
HUMBER STREET — — —	H. E. Plumtree
CLEETHORPES — — —	T. A. Humberstone
Gt. NORTHERN DEPOT *(Pasture St.)* —	R. Hufton
WALTHAM STATION — — — —	J. Croft
GREAT COATES STATION — — —	C. Smith

This was Edward Bannister's advertisement. The Grimsby Docks Office is just behind.

Edwardian photographers continued where their Victorian counterparts had left off. In this selection, from left to right, are a Marsden portrait, Edward Jeffray's advert, a Jenkins & Remy portrait of a sea-faring type, H. Jancowski's advert, a Lowthian portrait (hasn't the woman a distinctive perm?), Edward Mann's advert, an Audas portrait of a schoolboy, Pearson's advert and a Payne portrait of a young lady (note her wrist-watch!). There must be many albums gathering dust in the attics of old Grimsby family homes, where these and other examples of Grimbarian photographers' work abound in plenty.

1909 This was the *Poseidon*, a three-master, photographed by E.T. Jenkins. Later this year a six-master, the *Everett G. Griggs* from Victoria, British Columbia, was to visit Grimsby. She must have made a splendid sight.

Ice barques frequently used the Royal Dock up to the First World War, until the commercial production of ice in Grimsby killed this trade, and grain barges from the USA and Canada also moored here. Surprisingly, there was much wheat imported through Grimsby from Russia but the revolution put an end to that. The Royal Navy frequently moored here too, so that at any one time there could an assortment of vessels. (*Below*) The Alexandra Dock.

This was Harrison's Coffee Tavern and Hotel in Central Market. Henry Harrison made his reputation by designing a particular type of chimney-pot with a swivelling cowl, hence his nickname 'Potty' Harrison. He also sold china, just to confuse the issue, as can be seen from the shop windows.

Henry Harrison was born in Louth but made his fortune in Grimsby. When he died on 11 December 1930, aged eighty, he was the oldest serving member of Grimsby Borough Council and yet, curiously enough, was never Mayor.

The North Eastern Steam Fishing Company's tug-of-war team in 1910. They were raising money on behalf of the Orphans' Home. The company was owned by the Baskcomb family.

The First World War

On either side of the flamboyant and successful Grimsby fish merchant, Webb Shute, are two brothers who both served in the First World War in which a total of 2,100 Grimsby men lost their lives.

1914 On 10 August Kitchener wrote to the Lords Lieutenant of England and Territorial Force Associations asking for volunteers. Who better to know the fittest and most capable men in service than John Stirling, the Chief Constable? Stirling (seen here in full dress uniform, reminiscent of the Boer War) was Chief Constable of Grimsby from 1901 to 1931, in charge of the local constabulary as well as exercising a heavy influence in the Fire Service. The soldiers who volunteered and enlisted from Grimsby became known as 'the Grimsby Chums'.

1915 The 'Chums' were effectively the 10th and 11th Battalions of the Lincolnshire Regiment. This company, photographed at Brocklesby (their official training camp) was taken in early 1915 and shows Capt. W.S. Pratte and CSM Toby Atkinson. Sergeant-Major Atkinson had seen action at the bloody battle of Omdurman, when 10,000 Dervishes were killed and, although he was barred from going to France with the Regiment on 4 January 1916 because of heart problems, he became pivotal in training recruits, giving up his grocery business to become a regular soldier.

Curiously, Grimsby did not fear an invasion but, rather, those dreaded Zeppelins. Cleethorpes, Scunthorpe, Hull, Sandringham and Lowestoft were all hit along the east coast and, although some bombs were dropped on Grimsby, it survived relatively unscathed. This was *Punch* cartoonist, W.M. Haselden's version of the German threat. Many Zeppelins did not survive the North Sea crossing, especially on their return journey, and the life expectancy of a Zeppelin crew member was one out of every three trips!

Everyone did their bit. Here we see war badges being awarded to Grimsby Boy Scouts by Colonel H. Kendall Oram of the Manchester Regiment.

This magnificent photo of the 10th Lincolnshires, with Lt. Col. The Hon. George Heneage in the centre of the group, was taken outside Brocklesby Hall. Seated fourth from the left is Staff Sergeant Charles Stebbings (affectionately known as 'Stebbo'), who was the physical instructor at Louth Grammar School before the war. The 'Chums' fought in the Battle of the Somme between 1 July and 18 November 1916 – now known as one of the catastrophic episodes of the First World War. All this, and more is recorded in Peter Chapman's book, *Grimsby's Own – The Story of the Chums*, published in 1991.

1916 The proudest moment of the war for Grimsby was at the Battle of Jutland, when a sixteen-year-old lad, Boy First Class 42563 John Travers Cornwell, serving on HMS *Chester*, remained at his post and manned his gun, staying in the firing line, while all the gun's crew lay dead about him. Sadly he was mortally wounded himself and died on his arrival back in Grimsby on 2 June 1916. But young Jack Cornwell was awarded the Victoria Cross and this portrait of him was painted posthumously to mark the event. The artist touching up the damaged painting is Clare Finn, in 1979.

This was the crew of HMS *Northumberland*, weighed down with guns and ammunition.

1918 This was seaman Robert Abraham Dyke (born 1896), who served in the Royal Naval Reserve from 10 December 1914 to 1 December 1919. He survived three major naval battles during the First World War, including a skirmish in the Dardanelles and was photographed here in 1918. During the Second World War he enlisted as a Petty Officer/Engineer, serving on the *Bahram* (a converted seine-netter). He was killed on 3 April 1941 when the ship was attacked and blown up off Spurn Point. His widow died in the Doughty Road Almshouses.

1917 Numerous large houses and institutions were commandeered for the war effort to act as convalescent homes. Weelsby Hall, the home of the Sleight family, was just one example, but soldiers could be sent anywhere. Here we see Private W. Newman of the Lincolnshire Regiment (fifth from left, centre row) recuperating at Te-Hara House, Rugby.

1918 Because of secrecy restrictions during the First World War, this group of munitions workers (mostly women) could not be photographed until 1918. They worked at the Victoria Street shell factory. The reason for this photograph was the visit of King George V and Queen Mary on 10 April, which included a tour of the munitions factory. The King had visited Foster's Wellington Factory in Lincoln on 9 April, which made tanks, and the following day this factory, where they made 6 inch tank shells.

Between the Wars

1927   After the roaring twenties there was the General Strike of 1926, followed by the Depression. This wonderful photo portrays three of the eleven Webb children who had assembled outside their house in Hope Street – Gladys, Roland and Iris.

1919   After the First World War trade resumed and peace-time activities came to the fore. This was the view of Grimsby Royal Dock. The Victorian legacy of rail and sea could be seen to its best advantage. It took much necessary traffic off the roads, leaving the new-fangled motor car and omnibus to battle with their more traditional neighbour, the horse. Doig's Creek is just visible in the background.

Waiting to unload a ship in the Royal Dock. There is a gang of men just underneath the crane waiting to unload this cargo into railway trucks.

1923   The staff of the Pasture Street Goods Office – porters as well as office staff. The photograph was taken by Edwin Noble of 233 Freeman Street and the man standing behind the gentleman seated on the left is Les Howe, who became something of a photographer himself.

1939   In the early 30s the fishing industry was devouring approximately one million tons of coal per annum. When the new Fish Dock was opened, six coaling berths with three mechanical hoists were built. These could supply steam trawlers at the rate of 60 tons per hour.

1924   The highlight of the year was the 'Works' Outing'. This was the Port Master's staff picnic to Hampton Court of 1924 and, despite the warm sunny weather, one or two of the ladies refused to take their coats off. It is worth noting that, of the twelve women photographed, only three are not wearing hats.

1928 In July this photograph was taken, showing the Marshall Knott and Barker's timber yards. The new bascule bridge across Alexandra Dock had replaced the earlier 1873 Corporation swing bridge, which had always been troublesome. It was officially opened by Edward, Prince of Wales, later to become King Edward VIII. Note the photographers in the bottom corner, itching to capture a picture of this enigmatic royal. Incidentally, the bridge cost £55,000 – a considerable sum in the 1920s!

The other port of call for the Prince of Wales was Dixon's paper mills at West Marsh. Here we see the future King Edward VIII, accompanied by Mr Dixon, the Mayor, Cllr Leslie Osmond, and Lt. Col. Arthur Heneage MP, on his tour of the factory.

The firm had been started by Joseph Dixon (seen here) and was continued by his three sons, Cuthbert, William and Oscar. Over the years Dixon's paper mill gave employment to thousands of Grimbarians. It continued to trade under the Dixon family banner, responsible for two famous brand names in Bronco and Dixcel toilet paper, until 1972 when it was sold to Bowater-Scott.

1922 Henry Lewis Taylor (1860–1922), born in Bristol, arrived in Grimsby at the age of sixteen. He served his apprenticeship on the smack *Vigilant*, which belonged to his skipper uncle, William Dickinson. Then wealthy Thomas Bascombe, who ran 'fleeters' out of Grimsby, made him skipper of the brand new *Arthur & Ernest* with the chance of buying his own smack, *Fortunate*. Within three years, Henry Taylor was a smack-owner and, through a series of astute moves, built up a small fleet of his own. The Taylor Steam Fishing Company was formed in 1920. He was noted for his business partnerships with the Hopwoods and Doughtys. Henry Taylor died on 18 March 1922 at the age of 62 and was survived by his widow, Amy, and son, Charles.

Between the wars the Great Grimsby Co-operative store at the junction of Freeman Street and Garibaldi Street enjoyed much patronage. In 1897 the Great Grimsby Co-operative Society had purchased 121–123 Freeman Street with a bakehouse in Garibaldi Street for £8,130. If the tower looks familiar, there's a similar one just around the corner on the top of the Methodist Central Market in Duncombe Street.

1930 Les Howe enjoyed taking photographs of shop-fronts and, in particular, art deco examples. During the thirties this fad seemed chic and modernistic, although few now remain. This Co-op shop window on the corner of Garibaldi Street and Freeman Street caught his eye.

51

1923 Every lunchtime Les Howe would visit the Orwell Street Baths, to keep fit. At this time Howe was employed by the railway at the Pasture Street Goods Office, before being transferred to the Grimsby Docks Office. Not long after this photograph was taken the Orwell Street Baths were handed over to the Corporation on 6 April 1923 by the Fisherlads' Institute.

1928 Not everyone could afford to hire a charabanc or go on an organised outing. Here we see the staff of James Gee enjoying a day at Cleethorpes Swimming Pool. James H. Gee, the drapers, of 108 Freeman Street, were noted for their fine fabrics and cloth.

Although these ladies from the Royal Marine could afford the luxury, in the twenties charabanc parties were commonplace.

1934 This year saw the death of the Grimsby artist Herbert Rollett. Although he was a farmer's son, born just outside Gainsborough in 1872, he adopted Grimsby 'citizenship' when he became an apprentice grocer, eventually opening his own shop, known as Rollett's Five o'clock Tea Store. He was elected an Associate of the Royal Society of British Artists in 1927, exhibited at the Royal Academy a total of eight times and was the father of Kathleen Rollett, who was no mean artist herself.

1929 On the football front, Grimsby Town were doing well. This was the line-up in the 1929/30 season. Back row, left to right: Jock Priestley, Jack Prior, Charlie Wilson, Tommy Read (goalkeeper), Arthur Bateman, Herbert Woods (trainer) and Teddy Buck. Front row: Tim Coleman, Jackie Bestall (the great inside-forward), Joe Robson, Steve Coglin, Billy Marshall and Charlie Wrack. Grimsby Town were in Division I from this year until 1948, apart from the 1932/33 and 1933/34 seasons, when they slipped into Division II. Incidentally, George Tweedy (who replaced Tommy Read as the Mariners' goalie) played for England.

1932 Emulating the Mariners – this was the Nunsthorpe Boys' football team of 1932.

1937 This is Skipper Jim Whitcombe, the son of Thomas Rowett Whitcombe, who arrived from Greenwich back in the previous century. Thomas R. Whitcombe died in 1937 but his family continued fishing. Both of Jim Whitcombe's sons, Jimmy and Tommy, went to sea. The photograph was taken by J.J. Payne of Cleethorpe Road, Grimsby.

1937 Another great character was Tom Sleight, of 194 Heneage Road, not to be confused with either Sir George or Sir Ernest Sleight. Tom Sleight specialised in running seine netters and motor vessels. The firm was still operating from the Fish Dock in 1956 as Tom Sleight (Grimsby) Ltd, Fishing Vessel Managers.

1936 Some skippers were characters. This was Robert Ebbage Randall, who was born in Hull in 1890. He knew Grimsby well, firstly because he served his apprenticeship there and, also, as the skipper of the *Thomas Hardy* (a Hull-based trawler) from 1931 to 1936 he frequently landed his catch in Grimsby. Eventually he settled in the town after returning from a trip to Durban (South Africa) on the SS *Windsor Castle*. While in Durban he bought shares in a hotel. This photograph of little 'Bobby' Randall holding up a small Zulu boy was taken just outside Durban.

1936 There have been many fine Grimsby skippers but there have also been some dubious ones. Dod Osborne stole his seine-netter, the *Girl Pat*, in 1936. When he should have been fishing off the west coast of Scotland, he was in fact heading for Spain. He put in for supplies at the small Spanish port of Concubion, left with bills unpaid and also took on provisions at the naval station of Dakar (French West Africa) before finally being cornered off British Guiana by the Royal Navy. The *Girl Pat* then returned to England and was used as a tourist attraction at seaside resorts before ending her days in the Caribbean. In the meantime, Dod Osborne enjoyed celebrity status but it was short-lived.

1936 Freddie Frith, winner of the Junior TT race in 1936 on the Isle of Man, was a popular figure in and around Grimsby. Instead of joining the family firm of funeral directors based in Scartho, Freddie Frith chose to ride with Norton. Then came the Second World War and, after war service, he won the 350cc World Championship with Vellocette. Many people will remember his motor cycle shop in Victoria Street which always had a good selection of Italian bikes. Eventually he retired to St Mary's Park, Louth, where he died.

1935   On Empire Day, Dacia Chivers of Nunsthorpe School was chosen as the Grimsby May Queen. She is seen here in the centre of the picture. She would have had a busy year because of all the celebrations for King George V's Silver Jubilee.

Throughout the twenties and thirties, much emphasis was put on keeping fit. This was the Open Day display of gymnastics in the Nunsthorpe School quadrangle, a practice continued until relatively recently. The 'school in a garden' was opened in 1931 in the Numsthorpe Garden Estate.

1938   Cinemas were to enjoy their hey-day in the thirties. There were often long queues waiting to watch those extravaganzas that transported ordinary working-class people and their imaginations to a different sphere. This was the staff of the Regal Cinema in 1938, a year after it opened. The photo was taken by Spencer's Press of 236 Hainton Avenue.

Although the Aquarium was now open at Grimsby Zoo (off Augusta Street), its days were numbered.

1939 This will conjure up memories for people over a certain age: the Eleanor Street site of Wintringham School.

1937 This delightful photograph of the staff of Wintringham Grammar School enjoying their Christmas Ball in 1937, depicts Mr Wheatley, T. Wilson, T. Webb, P. Gaine, Mr Agar, G. Jamieson, M. Burton, A Johnson, R. Bull, J. Hayward, E.J. Worrall and Mr Cracknell.

1938 This was the Wintringham First XI in 1938. Back row, left to right: B. Watkinson, C. Readman, N. Chatterton, S. Jennison, A. Fitch, F. Fowler and E. Cole. Front row: J. Holden, B. Hyldon, F. Gill, Mr E.H.E. Wilson, N. Hallett, A. Horton and R. Brocksom.

Rumblings on the continent by Hitler's Nazi Party were felt in England. While one faction tried to sweep any adverse rumours under the carpet, another prepared for what they hoped would never happen. This was the Wintringham School OTC, using remnants from the First World War (including those old Lee Metford rifles) to practise with at their exercise at Strensall, York.

The one notable emergence in the twenties was Freeman Street as a shopping centre. This was the view looking towards Riby Square.

Before the NHS came into being, hospitals ran on public subscription and donations. This was a Carnival held in aid of Grimsby Hospital in about 1930.

The hustle and bustle of the streets can be seen in this photograph – and we think we have traffic jams today! Note the old tram in the distance. People brought their fare to market from all the surrounding towns and villages – the vehicles visible here are from Louth and Mablethorpe.

The Second
World War

1940 During the German *blitzkrieg* of November 1940 several unexploded bombs landed on Grimsby. This was one such at Wyndy Way, which No. 2 Bomb Disposal Squad had the task of finding in 1949.

On the right is Petty Officer Webb, who eventually captained a minesweeper during the Second World War. Both Webb and two of his sons, Harry and Kenny, were killed during the war. The other man in the photograph is Len Brown, nicknamed 'Gunner' after the war. 'Gunner' Brown achieved his nickname during the Cod Wars when an Icelandic Catalina flying boat fired at his trawler the *Grimsby Town* and injured one of his crew. Brown retaliated with his Schermuly lifesaving rocket-gun and hit the flying boat.

Many Grimsby skippers joined either the Royal Navy or the Merchant Navy. This was Robert Ebbage Randall in July 1940 at Rosyth.

1941 HMS *Grimsby* (990 tons) was sunk in the Mediterranean on 25 May 1941. There had been an HMT *Grimsby* during the First World War (a requisitioned trawler).

1942 Just as the troops needed feeding, so too did all the other services. This was a group of ATS cooks (the unsung heroines), from left to right: Violet Fowler, Marian Jacobs, Letty Lawley, Margaret Marshall and another.

1940 Like so many other towns and cities Grimsby was not really prepared for war. This was a fire-drill being enacted by the National Fire Service.

During those war years the rail network was so reliable that food could be sent by train.

1941 This was a public shelter in the Market in Freeman Street. It received a direct hit during a raid. It was a miracle that none of the 30 people inside the shelter at the time was badly hurt. It is just possible to see the old Co-op warehouse in the background.

1941 Another casualty of the raid was Bon Marche on Cleethorpe Road. This was all that remained of the elegant store illustrated below.

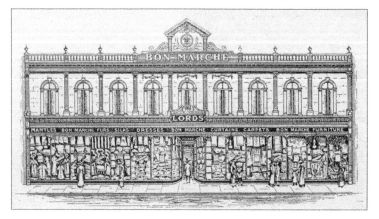

1941 This was the after-effect of a daylight raid on Humber Street, off Cleethorpe Road, on 27 February. Buildings were left like this sometimes for years after the war.

1943 The night of 14 June was particularly memorable for the residents of Grimsby. Incendiary bombs were dropped on Cleethorpe Road, Victoria Street, Central Market, Freeman Street and the Nunsthorpe Housing Estate. The following morning residents discovered 'butterfly bombs' all over the place – harmless-looking objects which could easily kill up to twenty people in a confined place. Warden Jack Oslear recalled an amusing incident concerning a man who found one of these bombs in his garden and took it to the ARP post in Sidney Park. Realising the seriousness of the situation, a Warden snatched the bomb and threw it away. It exploded, demolishing the new lavatory that the Wardens had been pressing for since the beginning of the war and which had only just been completed!

1943 The other band of unsung heroes were the fishermen who carried on fishing. It was spasmodic, but here we see a catch photographed on 10 January 1943 and then it was a question of scurrying back to port.

1943 The distinctive and ornate gates to People's Park were dismantled in this year. The idea was that they should be melted down and used for munitions. So, too, was the First World War tank, a valuable relic which stood in a corner of the park. Mayor Rudkin had listened to Mr Longley of the Ministry of Supply who, a year earlier, pleaded that 40,000 tons of steel were needed each week to supply the armed services. Other counties involved included Shropshire, Hampshire, Somerset and Durham, as well as Lincolnshire. Not only did the park gates go but, with them, thousands of iron railings, which were never replaced after the war. However, during the fifties, these same gates to People's Park lay in the Corporation Depot off Doughty Road but what happened to them after that remains a mystery. As for the iron railings from the fronts of houses, they were never used either. It was a governmental 'cock-up' – an all too familiar tale which we have continued to experience in the post-war period.

1942 The 5th Battalion of the Lindsey Home Guard, photographed at Springfield.

1941 Also using the ARC Service Club were members of the WVS (Women's Voluntary Service Corps), seen here enjoying afternoon tea! What is so fascinating about this photo is the ladies fashions – furs and and pill-box hats.

69

1943 Not all the bombs that were dropped on Grimsby went off. Here we see a group of men holding a bomb which had failed to explode in Legsby Avenue in July.

Regular concerts were given at the ARC (American Red Cross) Service Club for service personnel.

1944 Because life had to go on, there was even time to produce *The Merry Wives of Windsor* at Wintringham School. Included in the cast are R. Coulbeck, Roy Skaith, James Dobson, Roy Craske, Jack Newman, Evelyn Hickman, Paddy Bryant, Ian Halliday, Lorna Wilkinson, John Le Mesurer, Muriel Cousins, David Comins, Brian Cox, Tom Gamble, Tony Light, Mary Woodcock and Lindsay McNeill.

1945 There were many VE Day celebrations held throughout Grimsby on 8 May. Children were treated to sandwiches and cake while their parents looked on. This was one such, held in Scartho Church Hall.

1945 On 11 November Sir Walter Womersley, MP for Grimsby from 1924 to 1945, laid a wreath on the Cenotaph at Nunsthorpe. This white marble memorial cost £2,500, which was raised by public subscription, and was unveiled in 1921. The ground was donated by Lord Heneage, whose son Lt. Col. G.E. Heneage had commanded the 10th Battalion of the Lincolnshire Regiment in the First World War.

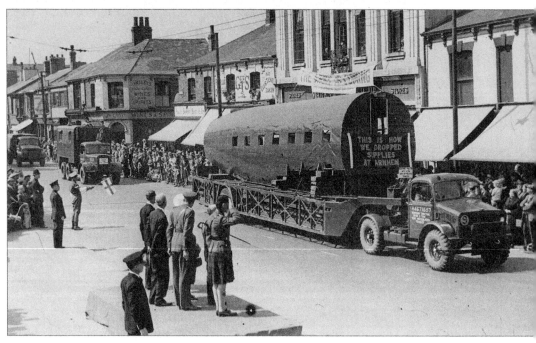

1946 'Operation Market Garden' may have been a fiasco but the plot was hatched in Lincolnshire and, after the war, here we see a convoy going down Freeman Street. The sign on the aircraft's fuselage says 'This is how we dropped supplies at Arnhem'. Note the old Marks & Spencer store, which was such a feature at one time, in the background.

The Postwar Period

When Grimsby people went back to peace-time occupations after the war, it was more often than not connected with fishing. Here we see some fishermen hauling in their nets. In those days a mine might inadvertently get caught up in the nets and occasionally there were accidents.

1948 After the War, many trawlers which had served as minesweepers reverted to their peace-time occupation once more. A plaque was placed at the foot of the Dock Tower on 20 May 1948 which read '1939–45 – A tribute to those who swept the seas'.

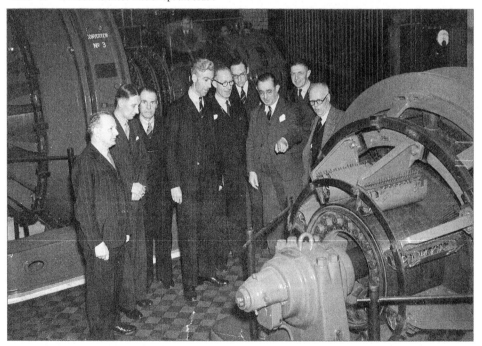

1948 Some members of Grimsby Council paid their last visit to the Corporation's Electricity Works in Moss Street before the hand-over to the Central Electricity Board on 1 April. Here we see a guided tour of the plant.

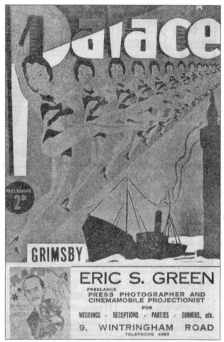

Mrs Meech, the skipper's wife, on board ship – an unlucky omen for most fishermen. She is seen here with the First Mate enjoying a bottle of stout! Note the bedroom slippers with zip.

1946 This programme for the Palace Theatre carries Eric Green's advert on the cover, with a caricature of the photographer himself. The programme was for *Three Waltzes*, which opened for the week 25–30 March with the likes of Iris Terry, Kendal Grant, Gerald Lennan, John Warwick and Lester Kay taking part.

At the bottom of King Edward Street, the corner fruit and vegetable shop used to advertise the Palace Cinema. This whole area was bombed in the Second World War. Only a few doors away was the old Oberon pub, which was once a popular rendezvous for skippers and their crews in the 1930s and early '40s. When the new Oberon was built, much of the old pub's character was lost.

1950 Skippers were invariably given nicknames – such as Horsehead Harrison, Soft Soap Sammy and Boiled Cod Charlie. Most were terms of endearment but occasionally they were not. Even the fittest of men had to be resilient to go to sea, not just physically but psychologically as well. This was Jimmy Evans caught in sunshine on a fag-break. Woodbines and Park Drive were the staple diet with most seamen!

When a catch was landed a pulley construction hauled the baskets to the lumpers. Note the ice, which is liberally scattered about and has fallen out of some of the baskets. It was the ice that kept the fish fresh.

Then the catch had to be weighed. Here we see a lumper cheerfully weighing his basket on scales that had obviously been used many times before.

1945 An example of those post-war catches, here we see some turbot caught in those bumper years just after the Second World War and photographed on 8 September 1945 on the Old Pontoon.

Most lumpers had a keen sense of humour. Note the cigarettes, or butt-ends. After the war you could not wish to meet a more cheerful soul than a Grimsby 'lumper', and their pay was good too!

1949 HRH Prince Philip visiting Grimsby. Before he visited the Docks, the Prince inspected a group of young cadets. It is Mayor Margaret Larmour who is holding on to her hat.

1947 This eighteen-year-old just missed the war but, like his father, still joined the Royal Navy during his National Service. Derrick Alan Dyke served with the Reserve Fleet at Harwich on a variety of ships and his last ship was HMS *Pembroke*. He left the Navy in April 1949. This photograph of him taken on board shows a raw young recruit who, on his return to Grimsby, worked on the Immingham railway. Sadly, he died on 20 January 1968, aged 40.

This wonderful moment of a skipper enjoying himself on shore-leave depicts Robert Randall in the garden of his house in Weelsby Road with his son Noel on one of those tricycles which were so popular in the 1940s. During the First World War 'Bob' Randall had been put in charge of a refrigerated barge, RB10, which was towed first to Plymouth and then to Gibraltar on its way to Gallipoli. It was carrying food to supply the troops at the Front. Going round the Bay of Biscay it was confronted by a German submarine, which torpedoed the tug (*Tigress of Bazra*) that was towing the barge and the crew were set adrift, landing in Spain before making their way back to England.

1950 On its maiden voyage the crew of *Northern Isles* were captured on camera. The ship GY149 (seen here) was built in 1950 for Northern Trawlers and eventually scrapped in 1976.

When their menfolk returned it was time for a celebration and off down to 'the local'. Here we see a collection of wives and sweethearts, including Marion Meech (second from right), toasting the safe homecoming of their husbands. I am sure someone will recognise the pub from the myriad of hostelries that surrounded the dock area.

1949 This photograph of Constance (Connie) Ward and Audrey Nicholson was taken at the back of 38 Brearton Avenue, Grimsby. The two boys are Clifford Ward (left) and Leslie Ward (right). What is so endearing about this photograph is the boys' coats, which will be familiar to people of a certain age.

Charles Ekberg joined the old *Grimsby News* as a reporter back in 1945 and worked on the *Grimsby Telegraph* from 1949 to 1953. In 1953 he joined the trawling paper, *Fishing News*, and soon became an authority on the fish trade, covering the 'Cod Wars'. He served on the Town Council from 1964 to 1970, although most people will probably remember his coverage of Grimsby Town's football matches on Radio Humberside. He was responsible for two books, *Grimsby Fish* and *The Mariners* (in conjunction with Sid Woodhead) – both were published by the now defunct Barracuda Books.

1949 Norma Whitcombe of Montague Street riding in a child's car. Despite rationing and the heavy debt that Britain had built up to the USA during those war years, these amazing toys were available to children, costing well over the average working man's weekly wage. Indeed, the few that survived are now worth considerably more.

1951 This aerial view of the Fish Docks shows the extent to which they had grown since the turn of the century. One of the new ocean-going trawlers is just arriving.

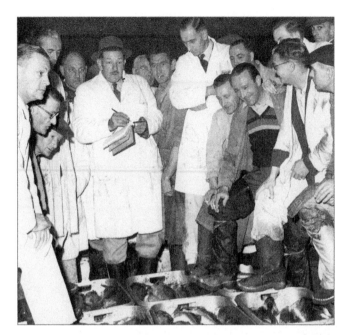

1950 Fish auctions were always busy in the fifties and, after the fish was auctioned off, usually to the various fish merchants, it then left to wend its way to various destinations throughout the UK.

One of the well-known Grimsby firms was George Sleight & Sons, fish merchants, named after Frederick George Sleight who turned to fishing instead of his family's traditional occupation of farming. After he purchased his first fishing smack he built up a trawling fleet of seventy-six ships which all sailed out of Grimsby. His fortune amassed including the purchase of Weelsby Hall, he was knighted in 1918 and made a Baronet in 1920. He was succeeded by his two sons, Major Rowland and Ernest Sleight.

1953 George Dawson was to the Fish Docks what Freddie Laker was to air travel. He promised the housewife cheap fish at a time when catches were high and courted Icelandic trawlers to land it for him. Dawson's plan of under-cutting the market lasted some nine months before it was nipped in the bud.

1953 At the Labour Party Fair held at St Stephen's Hall in April, the Hon. Kenneth Younger MP showed that pop stars were not the only ones to handle a guitar. He entertained several hundred people with his renditions, singing *She'll Be Coming Round the Mountain* as a finale. Younger was Grimsby's Labour MP from 1945 to 1959, was knighted and died in 1976.

1955 This was Ida Rosenburg, who lived in Peoples' Park, Grimsby, and will be remembered by many as something of a character. She was a Grimsby May Queen, did the European tour in her youth and eventually died in 1998. When Ida married she became Mrs Potts. In 1982 she had the dream of her lifetime come true when she was given the opportunity to drive a Rolls-Royce for the first time, albeit only for a few miles. Keith Sadler gave her the keys and she was to remark 'It was definitely easier than I thought' – it was also a lot different from driving her own Riley Elf!

But if the dress in the last photo was a tweed sui and the studio setting quite formal, this wonderfu snapshot (*c.* 1955) is quite the opposite. The flowin dress of Audrey Dyke (née Nicholson) draped ove the settee shows much imagination and (if you wi excuse the pun) much 'flair' in those otherwise dra fifties.

1957 Members of a hockey team from Wintringham Girls' Grammar School. (There are usually eleven players in a hockey team.) Back row, left to right: Diana Warman, Christine Dart, Jennifer Dean, -?-, Maureen Mooney. Front row: Rosalie Watkinson, Gibby Grampin, Trixi Pett, Rosemary Buxton. Curiously enough, *Blue Murder at St Trinian's* was made this same year, starring Alastair Sim and Joyce Grenfell.

1958 Catching a glimpse of the royal wave as Her Majesty the Queen and HRH the Duke of Edinburgh drive by on their way down to the docks, where they were met by Alderman Matt Larmour and his wife.

When people married in the 1950s it was usually for life; divorce was unheard of and illegitimacy almost a crime. Here we see a happy wedding party at the old Café Dansant.

Open Days down at the Docks were encouraged, when whole families looked over the ship where 'Dad' worked. By this time the large freezer-ships meant that fishermen could be away for weeks on end. There were three types of trawler: the ocean-going, middle-distance and seine-netter.

1957 Boston Deep Sea Fishing fleet moored on the North Wall. Their trawling operations were to end this year when they moved to Fleetwood in Lancashire.

Conditions had improved for fishermen in general but, towards the end of the fifties, the first 'Cod War' took place and the Royal Navy had to intervene to protect Grimsby fishermen sailing in foreign waters.

Both this photo and the last were taken on board the *Arsenal*, one of a fleet owned by Consolidated Fisheries and mostly named after football clubs. This shows men gutting fish and then throwing them into the washer before they were conveyed to the fish room in the hold.

This wonderfully expressive photograph of a fisherman gutting a fish encapsulates his profession. Those knives were razor-sharp, the boat was liable to rock at awkward moments and most fishermen bragged about how many fish they could gut in a minute. It needed every ounce of concentration so no wonder they invariably held a butt-end in their mouths!

Grimsby Dock Tower has always served as a beacon for home-coming sailors. The brick masterpiece of James William Wild (1814–92), which was based on a church tower in Siena, Italy, was built in 1852.

1958 This was the *Yesso*, built at Selby in 1958 for H.L. Taylor & Co. Ltd. It was sold in 1982 and re-named *Cleanseas I* when its job was to combat oil pollution in the North Sea. Eventually it was re-sold yet again in 1985 and, on its final voyage following Scott's route to the Antarctic, it became stuck in pack-ice and, like Shackleton's ship, was crushed and sent to the bottom.

1957   Allenby Chilton (the tall figure seen here in the centre of the picture) was player/manager for the Mariners from March 1955 to April 1959. After their promotion to Division II in 1956, Grimsby Town remained in Division II with Allenby Chilton at the helm.

These two giant gasometers, which were built before the Second World War at the back of Doughty Road, were further landmarks, although not as elegant as the Dock Tower. This unusual photo of Grimsby was taken from the 80ft extension of the Grimsby Gas Works Retort. It shows the neat rows of back-to-back terraced houses of which Grimsby was once so proud, together with the Moss Road Electricity Works building visible to the left of the first gasometer.

By the end of the 1950s Grimsby's Corn Exchange looked forlorn and forgotten. It resembled an isolated mausoleum, infested with pigeons and covered with grime from coal fires. With music emanating from Chambers' café, where the elderly trio played on, it had a surreal air. But what happened next took Grimsby by surprise!

Another area which is almost unrecognisable is between Victoria Street and Corporation Road. The Palace bar is just visible in the middle distance, as indeed is Spillers Mill (later called Marshall's Mill). This area was to undergo a complete revamp in the 1980s.

It meant that views like this one of the Old Market Place would be but a memory. This photograph of market day, when poultry and even pets in cages were auctioned, was taken in about 1930.

Swinging '60s and into the '70s

1963 The name of 'Ross' kept coming to the fore after the Second World War. Carl Ross had built up an empire beyond his wildest dreams. Here we see Ross House being erected in 1963 – it was opened by Keith Joseph in 1964 and the architects were Howard V. Lobbs & Partners.

By the time Carl Ross retired in 1968 his workforce totalled 15,000, he owned sixty trawlers and his annual turnover was in excess of £100 million. J. Carl Ross died in 1986, aged 84. His son John did not fare quite so well in business but his grandson David has made a fortune from mobile phones.

1960   The Freedom of Grimsby was conferred on the Fishery Protection Squadron of the Royal Navy. The ships involved included HMS *Duncan*, HMS *Malcolm*, HMS *Palliser* (which always seemed to make newspaper headlines), HMS *Belton* and HMS *Russell*. Captain H.H. Bracken (Captain of the Squadron) accepted the freedom scroll from Mayor Alderman R.S. Haylett in Peoples' Park in recognition of the Navy's action in the first of the 'Cod Wars' (1958–60). Afterwards the parade marched, with fixed bayonets and drums beating, to the Town Hall, where the Mayor took the salute.

1960   In March of this year the Riby Square taxi driver Mr Arthur Harrison, died. He had been a taxi driver for more than fifty years, starting work with his cabby father James Harrison, a partner in the Old Market Place firm of Burkett & Harrison.

1962   Occasionally fishermen were surprised when their nets were hauled aboard. On the *Northern Pride* this baby whale had become entangled. Originally the ship was owned by the Hull Ice Company after it was built in Germany in 1936. Then the *Northern Pride* saw war service before being transferred to Northern Trawlers in 1946. The boat was scrapped in 1964. Errant whales which strayed off course could be a nuisance to fishermen. Whales were even known to have come up the Humber Estuary and into the Trent!

1968 This year saw the death of Freddie Frinton. Freddie Hargate (his real name) was the son of a Grimsby fisherman who became well-known for the 'drunk' act, which lasted throughout his career. He is perhaps best remembered now for his television series *Meet the Wife* with Thora Hird, but not many people know that he was also a keen amateur photographer.

1964 In 1964 the Television Actor of the Year award was presented to Patrick Wymark, who was a familiar figure in and around Grimsby. Strictly speaking, he was a native of Cleethorpes (born there in 1926) but by the end of the 1960s he was known to millions as Sir John Wilder, the tycoon in *The Power Game*. His untimely death put paid to an otherwise budding career in films (*Doppelganger*) as well as his other many TV appearances, such as in *The Planemakers*.

1969 Grimsby singer Norma Procter. Born in Cleethorpes in 1928, she started singing at an early age in both the Scartho Methodist Church and Mill Road Methodist Church, Cleethorpes. Influenced by Kathleen Ferrier and, in particular, her performance of the *Messiah* by the Grimsby Philharmonic, Procter went on to study under Roy Henderson, Alec Redshaw (also pictured) and Paul Hamburger. Her rendition of the angel in Elgar's *The Dream of Gerontius* with Dr Slater in Lincoln Cathedral in 1957 was most memorable, as was her guest appearance at the Last Night of the Proms in 1974.

1967 One of the most extraordinary, indeed bizarre, episodes in pop history was Allan Smethurst – 'The Singing Postman'. Born in 1948 in Lancashire, educated in Norfolk and living in Cleethorpes, he composed his famous melody *Ha' You Got A Light, Boy?* along Grimsby's Victoria Street, where he delivered letters. He became something of a celebrity and a full-time entertainer, although his reputation was marred somewhat by an assault charge in 1976. Here he is being held aloft by players from the Grimsby Town Football Club.

1961 At the launch of the *Tokio* (which was built in Goole) we see, from left to right, Jack Piggott, Jaqueline Fenton, Ken Hopwood, Charles Taylor, Arthur Rutland, Lewis Doughty, a young Nick Taylor, -?-, Charlie Major, Marion Prestige, -?-, Mrs Phillipa Taylor, Jonathan Fenton, -?-, -?-, -?-, Lynn Hopwood (with Priscilla Hopwood just behind her). In the background, -?-, -?-, Carolyn Taylor, Mary Hopwood, -?-, Mr Craggs (the shipbuilder), Wendy Hopwood (now Bellamy), Basil Hopwood and Henry Taylor.

1962 A fine catch aboard the *Arsenal* (one of the Consolidated Fisheries' vessels – many of them were named after football clubs), shows just how tough their life could be. One slip by a rope could spell disaster. The *Arsenal* was to end its days in a breaker's yard at Fleetwood, Lancashire, in 1976, as some said a symbolic reminder of Britain's answer to the 'Cod Wars'.

1962 A Skippers & Mates Dinner at the Winter Gardens, Cleethorpes. Apart from Vic Hutchinson, the rest of this band were wives or girlfriends, mostly related to the Evans family.

1965 'Bunny' Newton went to sea at the age of fourteen and was a skipper by the time he was twenty-one years old. Nicknamed 'The Beast', because he often picked on sensitive souls and the weak, he was a natural-born fisherman with an instinctive ability to find the best catches. He was arrested by the Russians and Norwegians alike and adopted a buccaneering approach to life which hit the headlines in 1965 when his boat, the *Brandur* was impounded by the Icelandic authorities. Locking up three Icelandic coastguards in his cabin, he made a dash for the open sea and, but for the intervention of our own Royal Navy, he would have continued. He is seen here (second from right) with four of his brothers (left to right) Keith, Maurice, Binny and Derrick.

1964   This was a group of Grimsby Girl Guides being inspected by Lady Baden-Powell in July. Alice Babb is the Guide in the centre of the photograph.They were photographed at Market Rasen.

1968   The new library in Town Hall Square was opened on 15 September by the Rt. Hon. Anthony Crosland MP whilst the Mayor, Councillor T.W. Sleeman, looks on.

1969 On 28 May a group of pupils from St James' Choir School gathered in front of St James' Church before setting off on their school trip to Iceland. Grimsby is one of the few towns in England to have a choir school. They are normally reserved for cathedral cities.

1975 Alec Redshaw conducting members of the Grimsby Philharmonic Choir.

1968 This was the view looking down Cleethorpe Road from Riby Square before the flyover was built. Many familiar names such as Garrard's and the Lincoln Wine Shop have now gone.

1968 The view looking down Freeman Street. Again, many of the businesses have now gone including Smart's, Timothy White's and Clearvision. In fact, it is difficult to believe that so many businesses have changed hands in such a short time. The old Regal is still operating as the ABC.

1962 Despite their hard way of life, poor conditions and the stench of fish, most fishermen had a smile for the camera. Many of them accepted their happy-go-lucky existence, which could often be fraught with danger. Here we see two deckhands showing off.

1967 This view of Alexandra Dock shows the tower blocks looming in the background. When the Planning Department allowed these cold, impersonal blocks to be built, with names like Thesiger House and Garibaldi House, whole streets, indeed whole communities, were wiped out in the name of slum clearance.

1970   One of Grimsby's newest schools is Springfield School, Scartho. It opened in 1966. Here we see Class 1 of the Junior School with teacher Mr G. Holley. Back row: John Male, Neil Johnson, Alan Gerard, David Gladwell, Max Visholm, Stephen Parrott, Kevin Snell, Ernest Hayllar, Dereck Corrighan, Stephen Brown. Third row: Mandy Linford, Roslyn Hawkins, Kim Bradbury, Jackie Bramley, Lynn Walker, Teresa Gingell, Patricia Clarke, Sharon Cook, Susan Branston, Lesley Ward. Second row: Susan Fletcher, Susan Crowston, Beverly Carrington, Carol Jenkins, Margaret Malone, Karen Hallibone, Helen Fukes, Jean Hargraves, Janet Hodgson. Front row: Stephen Olsack, Dennis Bloomfield, John Grant, Grahame Clayton.

The Springfield netball team of 1971/72 comprising 4th year juniors. Back row, left to right: Reserve Corrina Hornsey, Jennifer Parkin, teacher Mrs Haigh, Carol Male, Linda Hammond, Reserve Dianne Jenkins. Front row: Julie Taylor, Jackie Grant, Patricia Larder (Captain), Gayna Beasley, Janine Sorrenson.

103

1978 Not all trawlers had a happy time of it. The *Okino*, seen here, was Japanese built and owned by H.L. Taylor's. It caught fire off the north-west coast of Scotland and had to be towed back to Grimsby with its Skipper Dave Venney. Chief Engineer Len Pye was badly burnt in the accident and the trawler was scrapped in 1979.

1979 Grimsby's reputation as a fishing port extends far beyond the confines of the North Sea. In 1975 Southern Ocean Fish Processors (Pty) Ltd, based in Albany, Western Australia, bought three Grimsby trawlers, the *Saxon Ranger*, *Saxon Onward* and *Saxon Progress* to fish the Great Australian Bight. The Grimsby crews who sailed with these boats subsequently settled in Australia.

Mr Norman Forster was so overwhelmed when he was presented with an inscribed tray and a table lamp that he had to sit down! Docks Manager, John Hughes, made the presentation while Personnel Officer Mr A. Shucksmith (second right) and Dock Master Captain W.E. Campbell (extreme right) look on.

1978 The Docks were still busy in the 1970s, as can be seen in this photo taken in July. The ship in the foreground is the *Rambler Rose* from Swansea.

Laurie McMenemy, Grimsby Town Manager from 1971 to 1973, won the Division 4 championship in 1972 which saw the Mariners move up to Division 3. He left Grimsby in 1973 to manage Southampton but was captured on film while paying a return visit in January 1978. Incidentally, the successful team that saw promotion in 1972 held a reunion dinner 21 years later at the Hainton Inn, Grimsby.

Of all the pubs in Grimsby, the one with the most fascinating name was the Oil Miller's Arms on East Marsh Street. Once one of the myriad of Hewitt's pubs (the Grimsby brewer), it closed its doors for the final time in the 1970s.

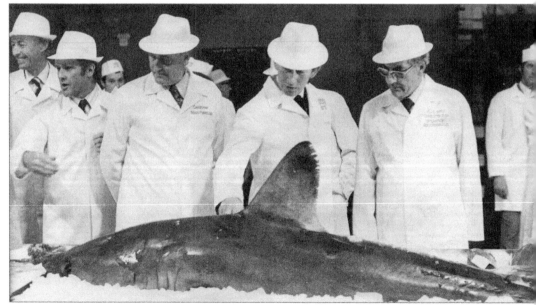

1978 A young looking Prince Charles came to Grimsby in 1978 when he visited the fish docks. Here we see him looking at a shark under the watchful eye of Mr Coulbeck.

Modern Grimsby

1982 Graham Dilley (the fast bowler) of Kent and England in action while Grimsby umpire Don Oslear looks on.

1980 Town fans go wild as Grimsby beat Sheffield United 4–0 and become champions of Division 3.

1984 On 8 February the children of Nunsthorpe Middle School were shown the town's civic insignia by Grimsby's Mayor A.J. Rouse. The teacher in charge of the class is John Cooper.

1983 Taking pride of place in the cricket pavilion of St James' School is this brass ship's bell, being rung by Christopher Hellyer. Aptly named the Jubilee Bell, commemorating the golden jubilee of St James' playing fields, it was donated by old boy Geoffrey Manchester of Pelham Road. The bell was cast from metal from HMS *Tiger*, which fought at the Battle of Jutland in 1916. The blond-haired boy (seventh from right), 'Snowy' Williams, is currently a Captain in the Royal Artillery.

1984 In October Austin Mitchell MP opened the First School Teaching Unit of Nunsthorpe School while the Mayor, Alexander Webster, looked on. The Headteacher of Nunsthorpe Junior was Ken Larder (seen here, seated, at the far end of the stage).

1985 On a lunch break, Peter Chapman views the fare of his local bakery in Freeman Street. Chapman, who wrote *Grimsby's Own – The Story of the Chums* (Hutton Press, 1991), already mentioned, and *Images of North Lincolnshire* (Breedon Books, 1993), was for a time the *Grimsby Evening Telegraph*'s reporter in Louth, where he was affectionately known as 'Scoop'. He went on to write his weekly column for the paper under the sobriquet 'Odd Man Out' and was responsible for the little-known *100 Years of the Grimsby Evening Telegraph*. He retired this year.

1987 In January of this year the subject of *This is Your Life* was the popular actress, Patricia Hodge. Although born in Cleethorpes. she spent much of her early life in Grimsby, where her parents ran the Royal Hotel, which closed in 1966. She attended St Martin's Preparatory School before moving on to Wintringham Girls' Grammar School. She is seen here surrounded by family and friends, including Irene Handl, John Hurt, Faith Brown and Nigel Havers, to name but a few.

1988 On 29 March the Princess of Wales visited Grimsby – seen here on a walkabout in King Edward Street, accompanied by Mayor David Casswell, where the Princess shook many hands. Also on this visit she officially opened Humberside International Airport, aided by Councillor Spooner.

1988 In April eight publicans staged a carnival weekend during which £3,700 was raised for Grimsby Hospital's Baby Care Appeal. Carnival organiser Gordon Taylor (licensee of the Angel Hotel) said, 'It was a fantastic weekend.' All the eight pubs that took part in the carnival were on Freeman Street.

1990 On 2 August Iraqi forces invaded Kuwait. The following year Operation Desert Storm took place to liberate Kuwait, during which time Flt Lt Simon Burgess of Grimsby was shot down and taken prisoner by the Iraqis. He is seen here after his release with his wife Nicola. Sadly, this Gulf War hero was to die in a tragic and unnecessary accident in Anglesey on 13 February 1996.

1991 This year saw the death of the Earl of Yarborough, seen here second from the left with Lady Yarborough, toasting the health of Mr Farrow while other members of the Brocklesby Hunt look on.

1988 A woman in a man's world (or are men in a women's world? – you can't be too sure these days): the Mayor of Grimsby, Sarah Campbell Woodliff looks wistful as she is handed a drink by Robin Chadburn (Chairman of Mansfield Breweries) at the West Marsh Club. George Jackson (third from left), President of the club, had at this time been a member for 42 years.

1990 As the turn of the century approaches it will be up to these children to carry the mantle of their parents, grandparents and great-grandparents. This was Lisle Marsden Church of England Aided Infant School. Recognisable are, back row, Vanessa Gooseman (4th from right), Fay Walton (4th from left); second row from back, Jamie McCree (2nd from left), Steven William (5th from left); third row from back, Adam Randall (2nd from left), Ben Cowley (4th from left), Carla Mumby (3rd from right); front row, Adam Blanchard (3rd from left), Adam Cousins (4th from right) and Adam Burrow (extreme right). The school was named after the Revd Canon E.L. Marsden, (Chairman of the Board of Governors of St James' School in 1936). Incidentally, the Headmistress was called Mrs Thatcher at the time this photograph was taken.

1991 In the 1970s and '80s snooker became a major television sport. One of its stars was Mike Hallett, who married Janet Hearing in June. Suddenly Grimsby was awash with snooker stars such as Gary Wilkinson, John Parrott, Stephen Hendry, Nigel Bond and the rest for this special event.

Skipper 'Bunny' Newton was one of the most colourful of all Grimsby skippers and rarely out of the limelight. He retired at just the right time, drove a Rolls-Royce, invested wisely in bingo halls and racehorses and even opened a nightclub in Cleethorpes called 'Bunny's Place'. Seen here with two of the stars of the popular BBC series, *It Ain't 'Alf 'Ot, Mum*, Windsor Davies and Don Estelle, Newton made the newspaper headlines for the last time when he was murdered on 10 July 1991, shot dead by his son.

Norman Lamont shot through the ranks of the Conservative Party to become Chancellor of the Exchequer under John Major. Although not a Grimbarian by birth, Norman Lamont originally moved to Welholme Road in 1953 after his father was appointed Casualty Surgeon at Grimsby General and the family have made it their home ever since. Lord Lamont now sits in the House of Lords.

1992   Janet Tierney (right) signing copies of her book *Around Grimsby* in December. At this time, Janet Tierney (formerly Janet Swithinbank) was Curator of the Welholme Galleries. She wrote three books on Grimsby, including *Grimsby in Old Photographs*, *Around Grimsby* and *Grimsby Docks* (all published by Sutton Publishing) as well as *Cleethorpes As It Was*, in 1984.

1992   On 16 January, Princess Anne visited Grimsby to open the Ross Young's pizza factory, South Quay. She is seen here on a walkabout.

1993 In July, at the Open Day on Grimsby Fish Dock, *Emmerdale* star, Chris Chittell (alias 'Mr Nasty' – Eric Pollard), comes face to face with a giant cod held by Minnow Fish director Jack Benzie.

1993 The Grimsby actress Julie Peasgood, second from left, was educated at Wintringham School, the daughter of a welfare officer for the National Dock Labour Board. She is seen here at a school centenary reunion with former classmates June Mansfield, Lindsey Osborne and Janet Bygott.

All-important parts of any football team are its mascots. Here we see the Mariners' choice of three young lads, Sean Borrell, Richard Hubbert and Danny Rees, with Town skipper Paul Groves (extreme right) and Tranmere's captain, John Aldridge (extreme left), before their game at Blundell Park.

117

1994 The start of Grimsby's new £13million Fish Dock can be seen in this aerial view. Constructed on the site of the old No. 1 Market and Dock, tons of sand have already been used as in-fill, upon which the new market hall, trawler landing area and ancillary buildings would be built, hoping to attract trawlers from all over Europe.

1991 Instructor Betty Lister shows youngsters Adam Randall and Alex Willcocks how to make a ship's wheel from cor dollies at the Welholme Galleries in Grimsby. The ship's wheel was at one time the symbol of Grimsby's wealth.

1995 Celebrating the anniversary of VE Day in Heritage Square is Dot Smith (seen here) with her picture of Sir Winston Churchill.

This was 'Miss Grimsby Evening Telegraph', Yvette Driver, photographed in a nostalgic mood at The Party Box, Grimsby.

1998   St James' choirboys singing at the Fish Docks during their annual Christmas visit on 18 December.

Ships berth at the new Pontoon. At the beginning of the last century Grimsby was the greatest fish port in the world and there is the National Fishing Heritage Centre to remind us of past times, but I wonder how the town will fare in the next century.

ACKNOWLEDGEMENTS

First of all, I would like to thank the *Grimsby Evening Telegraph* for all their help in putting this volume together, particularly Peter Moore, Peter Chapman, Peter Craig and Linda Roberts, whose guidance was invaluable. I should also like to thank Henry and Nick Taylor, Noel and Bev Randall, Mike Surr, Tim Dixon, Tom Whitcombe, Steve Jackson, John Callison and Rachel Ettridge of Grimsby Town Hall, Andrew Tullock of the Welholme Galleries, John Wilson of North East Lincolnshire Archives and the Mayor, Councillor Hyldon-King, for allowing me to use the Grimsby coat of arms. Last, but not least, Louth Secretarial Services for typing the manuscript so carefully.

MAYORS 1900–95

1900 Harrison Mudd	1933 Cornelius Canning	1966 William James Molson
1901 Moses Abrahams	1934 John Hogg	1967 Alfred Henry Chatteris
1902 Francis Evison	1935 John Wales Prior	1968 Thomas Walter Sleeman
1903 Anthony Bannister	1936 Thomas Sylvester Stone	1969 Alfred Cyril Parker
1904 Joseph Hewson	1937 Charles Edwin Franklin	1970 William Ernest Wilkins
1905 Frederick William Riggall	1938 Henry Weldrick	1971 Lilian Trayer
1906 Jacob Pickwell	1939 John Joseph Sutton	1972 Florence Elizabeth Franklin
1907 Thomas George Tickler	1940 Charles Henry Wilkinson	1973 Margaret E. Darley
1908 Frank Barrett	1941 James Keay	1974 Matthew Quinn OBE
1909 Robt Wm Roberts	1942 Edward Shaw Rudkin	1974 Ivor Hanson
1910 James Whitley Wilkin	1943 Max Bloom	1975 Alfred Neilson
1911 Alfred John Knott	1944 Charles William Hewson	1976 Peter Ellis
1912 Christopher Miller	1945 William Roberts	1977 Peter Willing
1913 John Henry Tate	1946 John William Lancaster	1978 Marjorie Elliott
1914 James William Eason	1947 William Banks Bailey	1979 Chesney Aubrey Brocklesby
1915 Thomas Campbell Moss	1949 Margaret Larmour	1980 Walter Banyard Smith
1916 Joseph Barker	1950 William Henry Windley	1981 Roy Bannister Cheeseman
1917 Frederick Moss	1951 John Ashcroft Webster	1982 Roy James Ellis
1918 Frederick Moss	1952 George Cedric Wilson	1983 Anthony Jack Rouse
1919 John William Hobbs	1953 George Herbert Atkinson	1984 Alexander Mackie Webster
1920 Franklin Thornton	1954 Wilfred Harris	1985 Anthony Frederick Coleman
1921 Joseph Henry Curry	1955 John Cornelius Bernard Olsen	1986 Pauline Frances Ellis
1922 Walter James Womersley	1956 Wilfred Harris	1987 David Charles Casswell
1923 Richard Guy Kitching	1956 Matthew Quinn	1988 Sarah Campbell Woodliff
1924 Frank Barret	1957 John Henry Franklin	1989 David Andrew Currie
1925 Ernest Harrison	1958 Matthew Larmour	1990 Helen Douglas Hooton
1926 Leslie Kingsford Osmond	1959 Fred Goodfellow Gardner	1991 Kathleen Phoebe Bell
1927 Leslie Kingsford Osmond	1960 Reginald Swan Haylett	1992 Noel Granville Perkins
1928 Malcolm Guy Smith	1961 George Herbert Pearson	1993 Stephen J. Norton
1929 Isidore Abrahams	1962 Elias William Marshall	1994 Alec Bovill
1930 Alfred John Knott	1963 Cyril James Moody	1995 John B. Colebrook
1931 Charles William Dixon	1964 Jean Baxter Baillie McLaren	
1932 Thomas Newby	1965 Denys Eugene Petchell	

Printed in Great Britain
by Amazon